ENOUGH

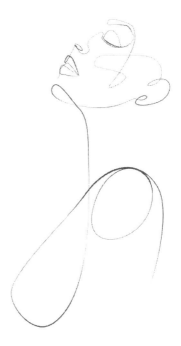

ISBN: 978-1-9992579-1-0

Printing, 2021

Blue Heart Publishing

For more information, please visit
www.ShopMsSosa.com

Dedicated to all the women that have suffered heartbreak, have lost their worth, have chased someone that wasn't good for them, who knew they deserved better and are fed up of staying silent. You're not alone, and you'll overcome everything you're going through. Enough!

These are my past experiences with a few of my exes. I hope you can relate. xoxo

- M. Sosa

Healing is messy. There will be good and bad days. Many days reminiscing on what you could've done to change the outcome and other days when you're happily living your best life. There will be moments where you feel you're completely over the heartbreak and random moments where it hits you all over again. Through it all, remember that you're human. It's normal to feel, to break down, to smile… to take all the time you need to move on.

You keep putting yourself
through the pain of fighting
for someone who's shown you
several times that they don't care.
When will you stop hurting yourself?

To heal from the damage of a narcissist, you'll have to quit blaming yourself for what happened. They convinced you that your reaction to their abuse wasn't normal and that you were imagining everything bad that happened. They thought they had the right to mistreat you, and that you had no right to stand up for yourself. They were wrong. They never blamed themselves for their shitty behavior because in their eyes, they were always right and when you finally decided to leave, they created stories to make you sound like a monster. Whatever they said about you, you got out and that's something to be thankful for. Your healing will be a day-to-day process that will take you through a rollercoaster of emotions. Eventually, you'll need to trust yourself again, and you'll need to put down the idea that the abuse was your fault. Self-blaming yourself won't help you heal. Accept that you may never get the closure you want from them because it has to come from within. But most importantly, remind yourself that you're not a victim. You're a survivor and everything that's coming will be the breakthrough you've been waiting for.

You did what you had to do to keep your peace of mind. You got fed up with their lies and constant manipulation. You gave them chance after chance to make things right. You endured countless moments of neglect when you needed them most but through it all, they never made any effort to fix what was broken. Stop feeling guilty. If that person kept doing what they clearly knew was hurting you, they didn't respect you. Time to move on.

People don't change.
They modify their behavior for who they want to.
If they're constantly showing you that they don't
care—they don't care. Period.

They know you deserve more and if you
find it, you'll move on. So, they keep you hanging
on by a thread in hope that you'll keep holding on
to them. They keep breaking promises and act like
they care only when they feel they're about to lose
you. They manipulate you into believing that you
need them, but they need you to fuel their fire. The
moment you decide to let go will be the moment
they lose control over you. Only you have the
power to stop the madness.

A brand new you is waiting to emerge
from all the pain you've endured.

Let it flow through you and break free.

Run from anything that makes you question
your worth or makes you feel as if you're
struggling to breathe. You shouldn't
feel like you're drowning.

Sometimes, the only solution is to let go.
No more overthinking. No more crying.

No more headaches. *Exhale*, keep your sanity.

I know you desperately want to make
things work. You've given your all to them
and you feel they owe you the world for everything
you've done, but the truth is they don't owe you
anything. Your hopeless desire to change them is
overpowering the reality of what you're both
feeling. They're not reciprocating the same love
because they don't feel the same way you do. If
someone keeps showing you they're not into you,
take it for what it is. Open your eyes and see the
truth in front of you.

Just because you decided to end
things doesn't make you a bad person.
You're allowed to cut ties with anybody
that's threatening your peace of mind.
Whether it's a friendship, relationship, or
family member, you have the right to do what's
good for you. Nobody can tell you otherwise.

Sometimes, you outgrow people.
You may still love or care for them, but their part in your story is over. You're in a different place in your life and certain things that you used to focus on are meaningless now. The way you see life has changed. Your goals aren't aligned with people from your past, and you know you need to cut ties with them to move forward. There's nothing wrong with growth if you're doing it for you... and only you. Never dim your light because you want to please others. Keep growing. Keep pushing forward. Keep reaching for the stars.

Dear Self,

I know you've been hurt. I know it's been a tough journey and you feel as if nobody understands what you're going through but you're not alone. Hang in there. In the meantime, don't run back to old ways just because it feels comfortable. Stop chasing people that don't want to be caught and let go of the idea that you must be the same person you were a year ago. Everything you're going through is preparing you for something better.

You've worked so hard to become
the person you are today. Never let others
intimidate you into believing that you're not
worthy of reaching your full potential. Those
that come into your life and try to bring you
down are there to teach you about the type of
people that shouldn't be in it. You're stronger
than you give yourself credit for. The moment
you realize that will be the moment things
change in your favor. Never dull your shine
because others don't want to see you sparkle.

There's only so much you should tolerate from anybody that's playing mind games with you.

One time might be an accident.

Two times might be a coincidence.

Three times is definitely a pattern.

Your body is surrounded by a field
of constantly changing energy,
and anybody you come in contact
with that has negative energy will pass
that onto you. It can cause you to feel
anxious or upset. That's why it's important
to keep negative people away from you.
Detach yourself from energy that isn't yours.

Stop bending over backwards
trying to protect someone else's feelings.
They're not holding back their words,
so why are you staying silent, taking in all
the hurtful shit they're saying to you?

Boundaries... Boundaries... Boundaries.

When someone treats you like an option,
remove yourself from the equation and
don't look back. You deserve to be number one
and not someone's booty call whenever they
get bored or need something to rub up on.

I haven't felt like myself lately.
There are good days and there are bad ones.
There are moments where I fall apart and
others where I feel I can conquer anything.
Through every emotion possible, I keep
reminding myself that I'm human. It's okay
to have shitty days and it's even more
okay to take a break from the world.

Remind yourself that this isn't the end.
The pain won't last forever. You may not
feel it now but eventually, you'll understand
why things happened the way they did, and
you'll be glad that you pushed through it all.

I just wanted closure from you. I wanted to hear
the reason why you left. I wanted answers,
anything to ease my mind and my heart. It took me
years to realize that no matter what you said or did,
it would be pointless because I wouldn't believe
your explanations anyway. The desire for closure
was holding me back from moving forward. I had
to let go of the desire of hearing you admit you
were a complete jerk, and wrong for hurting me
how you did. The only closure I ever needed was
in me. That's when I finally found peace of mind.

The right attention from the
wrong person will get you in trouble.
Never let loneliness keep you in the arms
of someone who isn't good for you.

I don't miss the lies, the disrespect, the disappearing acts or carrying 100% of the relationship on my shoulders.

The things I used to tolerate in my past relationships are things I will never put up with again.

Not having to question someone's
loyalty is what you deserve. Don't settle for
mediocre type of relationships that have you
second-guessing everything about them.

One of the biggest lessons I learned
was to stop wasting my time waiting
for someone that was unsure about what they
wanted. No point in losing years of your life
pursuing someone that doesn't realize your worth.
Leave now and save yourself the headache.

Be your authentic self and never
let others dictate how you should
act or be. Laugh, love, prosper and live.
Surround yourself with people who are
genuinely happy to be around you.

Toxic people will make you feel as if you're worthless. They'll target your self-esteem, and they'll try to make you feel small every chance they get. They'll ignore your boundaries and they'll disregard your feelings because they know you won't defend yourself. They won't regret anything they're putting you through because in their eyes, they've done nothing wrong. Stop making yourself available to people that don't have your best interest at heart. If your boundaries upset them, let them go. Kick them to the curb. Don't let them to ruin your life. You can't improve your life if you keep surrounding yourself with negative energy.

If chasing someone isn't mutual,
change direction or better yet,
don't chase them at all.

To the woman reading this right now with
tears rolling down her face—I was once you.
Your heart is heavy and a part of you feels numb.
I know what it feels like to want to pick up the
phone and call the person that broke you down,
or send them a text while hoping they'll reply,
even though you know they won't. I know how
hard it is to walk away from the memories you
shared because a part of you wants to hold on
when you know you should be letting go. I know
what it's like to spend lonely night waiting for
them to come back, hoping they'll give you one
more chance, but they never do. I also know
what it feels like to let go of all the confusion
and heartbreak, and realize they weren't worth
your tears. I hope you find the courage within
you to realize you're worth so much more than
what you're settling for. The right person won't
make you feel as if you're not good enough. You
were always worth it. Don't give up on yourself.

I used to worry about what you felt after
our breakup instead of worrying about what
I was feeling at the moment. You were more
important than me. What I felt didn't matter,
even though you're the one that tore us apart.
I thought if I focused my energy on you,
somehow, you'd come back to me. What a
foolish person I was then. That's something
I promised to never be again.

You can't save people.
It's not your job to save anyone.
They have to want to help themselves.
Let them rewrite their own story.

It's going to take as long as it takes
to get over your breakup. There's no magic pill
or cure to make it go any faster. Give yourself
grace because it's the loving thing to do and
also accept that you won't end up hurting
forever. Everything will pass.

In the meantime, *live*. Quit wallowing in the
hurt. You have so much more to see.

It's not about them changing.
It's you that needs to wake up

and needs to learn to *leave them alone*.

Your love is gold, and they want pebbles.
Why spend so much energy on someone
who doesn't care what you're feeling?
It's a waste of time. You're damaging
yourself in the long run. If they're not willing
to love you the right way, why keep waiting
and hoping that they'll change their mind?
Let them go and free yourself from the toxicity.

You're doing all the right things to feel good but sometimes, the pain lingers. Everything you're feeling is normal. Nobody should expect you to be 100% when you have emotional baggage you're trying to get rid of. There's no set timeline to healing, so be easy with yourself and take as long as you need to move on.

We all mess up at some point in our lives.
We all make mistakes. That's the point of
being human. You won't always have the
best judgment and you might do things
you regret doing but learning from those
mistakes will help your growth. Every regret
in life has a lesson to be learned.

Reality check:
Losing them wasn't a loss. It was a win.
If they cheated, treated you like shit, consistently
lied or made you feel as if you weren't enough,
be thankful they're no longer in your life.

I know you wish things had turned out
differently but it's important to accept
what happened and realize that sometimes,
things happen so better things
can come into your life.

Letting go of my ex was one of the toughest things
I've ever had to do. I loved him with every inch of
my body and soul. He was my everything. The one
I wanted to grow old with. The one I was supposed
to have children with. The one that promised me the
moon and the stars, but life has a funny way of
working out because what I thought I wanted back
then isn't what I want now. And even though I spent
years wondering why things happened the way they
did, I'm thankful because if they didn't, I wouldn't
be the person I am today. What I used to put up with
before are things I will never allow in my life again.
Trust the process. Stop spending so much time
worrying and crying over the loss of a relationship
and realize that some things weren't meant to be.
What's meant for you will find you and what
isn't will fade away.

I know it's hard to believe
but one day you're going to wake up
and he won't be the first thing on your mind.

Sometimes, you have no choice but
to leave all the drama and heartache behind.
When you've tried and tried, and tried again,
and nothing changes, you have the right
to choose happiness above anything else.
Leaving won't be easy but it'll be worse if you
stay with someone who's bringing you down.
Your mental health matters and anybody
affecting it should be removed from your life.

If they loved you, you wouldn't
be crying over them the way that you are.
You wouldn't be questioning where things
went wrong. You wouldn't be up late at
night wondering if they're missing you, too.
You wouldn't feel as if you've given them
the world and you have no place in it.
That's not what love feels like.

Never allow the person that hurt you
be the reason you end up having sleepless nights.
They don't deserve your energy. They shouldn't
keep you feeling stuck. Your time is valuable
and shouldn't be wasted on someone that doesn't
care what you're going through. Your happiness
matters. Let them go and keep moving forward.

You won't always be right.
You won't always have the right answers.
You may not know where you're headed.
But believe that things will eventually
make sense. You'll end up where
you're supposed to be.

They betrayed your trust, and you find it hard to concentrate on anything other than your turmoil and pain. Some days will be easier than others but don't give up. Feel your emotions and avoid keeping them bottled in. Take your time to heal from what others have done to you.

Self-care means spending quality time
with yourself. Go to a spa and get a mani-pedi
done. Go to a salon and get a new haircut or
change your hair color. Join a yoga class and let
yourself go. Go to the movies alone. Take a
break and listen to your favorite playlist. Relax
and unwind with a good book. Take a long and
much needed bubble bath. Make sure you do
something for yourself and that it puts a huge
smile on your face. This is your moment.
Do something that brings you happiness.

I hope you meet someone
that shows you what true love
feels like and isn't afraid
to show it with their actions,
not only their words.

We often warn others about red flags
but what about green flags in a relationship?
Being able to be yourself unapologetically,
laughing out loud, respecting one another,
showing affection, communicating without
fear of consequences, aiding in your growth
process and willing to compromise while setting
your own boundaries are some of the signs
you're with someone that genuinely cares for
your well-being. If your partner isn't doing
any of those—RUN.

Truth hurts when you know
someone isn't good for you.
You want to believe they're "the one"
but you know deep down inside that
they're never going to change or
give you the love you deserve.

To anybody who's reading this,

I hope that whatever is clouding your mind disappears and all the stress you're feeling goes away. Overthinking will destroy you if you don't put your mind at ease. So, take a step back, relax and let your confusion fade. Let peace and love enter your body, and let it calm your soul.

You're restless because you're allowing
your thoughts to take over your mind.
You're overthinking every situation and
it's driving you crazy because you're trying
to find answers to things that are out of your
control. You're hurting yourself by not letting
your mind rest. Take a step back and let yourself
breathe. Take in what's happened, accept
that you can't change the outcome and
believe that better things are coming.
Find peace in the chaos.

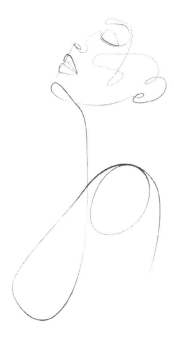

Learn to be okay with things not working out.
Learn to be okay with people not wanting to be
around you, excluding you or ignoring you.
They have the right to say if something or
someone isn't for them, the same way
you have the right to do the same.

When did I become so desperate for your love? I was trying to hold onto you, even though you had already let go of me. I needed to see you, to feel you, to hear you... I was trying too hard to win you back. I didn't love myself to realize that I was the problem, and I had to get rid of this obsession by accepting that you would never be mine again. My future wasn't going to be with you and as tough as it was to admit it to myself, I had to let you go. I had to let go of the idea of what could've been and focus on what was happening in the present.

Breakups are hard. There's nothing easy about someone leaving. The person you would turn to for love, comfort and security is gone and now you have to start all over again. The feeling of distress is hurting you because the person that's usually helping you deal with the good, the bad, and the ugly, is not here to help you deal with this loss. But you know what? You're going to be fine. Rejection is a blessing because you never know what it's protecting you from and everything that feels as if it's destroying you now will eventually fade away. Trust your journey, even the detours and delays.

You should know the things that bother me by now. All the arguments about the same things but nothing ever changes. The empty promises you keep making that never get fulfilled. The lies you tell me to keep me holding out for hope. I keep holding you down whenever you need anything but all we do is go round and round, lying to each other that things will be okay when we know that things aren't going to work out. All you want to do is play with my heart and you think I'm going to stick around while you keep playing around. You're not the man I thought you were. Pack your stuff and get out. Enough with the games, I'm too grown for childish behavior, and I won't tolerate your shit anymore.

If there's one thing that strikes a nerve, it's when someone starts to care for you when it's too late. Why couldn't you love me back then? Why couldn't you see how good I was for you? Why couldn't you swallow your pride and say "I'm sorry" when I needed it? Why couldn't you make as much effort as I did? Why couldn't you fight for us when I was struggling by myself?

Answers that I'll never get and no longer need.

I'm good, love. *Next.*

Before I gave up on you, I gave it my all. I tried and tried, and tried again, to help you fix what was broken between us. You never cared and would shrug it off as if I was exaggerating, as if I was making a big deal out of nothing. That broke me down further. I was scared of being alone because I wasn't sure how I would function without you, when you were all I was used to. And then it hit me, you gave me the best gift of all, a new perspective. I didn't want to feel disappointed, neglected, and unloved anymore. I didn't want to feel as if anything I did wasn't good enough because I deserved to be happy, and that meant not settling for crumbs when I could have the whole cake. If you weren't going to make the effort, then I was going to do it for myself by walking away from someone who would never see my worth.

Bitter. That's the perfect word to describe how I felt when I heard you had moved on. How are you going to throw it all away? Mad at the fact that she was doing all the things we used to do. Mad at the fact that you were spending all your time with her. Mad at the fact that she was building a future with you. It took me years, but I got over it by forgiving myself and letting go of the idea that we had a chance of reconciliation. Deleted all your pictures, blocked your calls/texts/social media accounts and left no trace of us around me. One of the wisest decisions I've ever made. I'm happier and in a better place mentally, emotionally, physically and spiritually. Thank you.

Face reality. Look at yourself in the mirror
and ask yourself if you're genuinely happy.
Ask yourself if this is what love is supposed to feel
like. The faster you realize that this isn't love, the
faster you'll move on. Someone that's into you will
always show you with their actions, not their words.
They'll let it be known that they want you to be in
their lives and won't hesitate to show you that
you belong there.

Stop making excuses for them. If they're showing
you the complete opposite, be realistic and let them
go. Give yourself the opportunity to heal
and move on.

The greatest moment is finding the courage to
let go of everything you can't change and
realizing that it was holding you
back all along. Free yourself.

I was never ready for you to leave
but after putting myself back together,
rebuilding my self-esteem and accepting
that life goes on without you, I realized it
was the best gift you could've given me.
I'm stronger than I was before, and I'll
never beg anybody to stay again.

Whatever turmoil you're feeling,
feel it fully but don't give up on yourself.
You're being redirected towards
something greater.

You never needed anybody
to complete you. Everything you
ever needed was hiding in you all along.
Everything you've been searching for is
a part of you. Look deeper.

You may feel broken but you're beautifully
broken. You're a warrior and you'll get past
your traumas, one day at a time.

Strong women never give up.
We fight until there's nothing left to fight for.
We help others even if we're going through
something. We don't let little bumps on the road
get the better of us because we know whatever
comes our way, we'll get past it. We always find
a way to come back stronger than ever.

You shouldn't sugarcoat how you're feeling because you're afraid your partner will get upset. If something is bothering you, say how you feel. What's the point of being with somebody you're scared of being honest with? Keep being genuine. Keep being honest. When you're in a good, healthy relationship, your partner will listen to you, and they'll take what you said to heart. They'll work on fixing the problem with you. The wrong person will get angry, throw a hissy fit or will completely ignore what you said.

I'm far from perfect but I won't allow
anybody to abuse me again. I'm worth it.
I always have been and always will be so
lowering my worth for anyone is
something I'm not willing to do.

Messing around with people
who aren't good for you will cause you
heartache and pain. When you see one red flag,
another one usually appears. Ignoring them will
be your downfall. Break things off before
you're stuck wishing you had left sooner.

If you're not supporting my growth,
you're using up space that could be given to
someone else that will. Buh-bye.

I'm done. I kept giving you chances
you didn't deserve. I fought and fought
to make things work. I thought I had to
keep trying harder each time things fell apart
until I realized, I was fighting on my own.
You no longer made me a priority in your life,
so I had to change your role in mine.

Never blame yourself
for someone else's lack of appreciation.
They don't know what they're missing out on.

Nobody can take away what's meant for you. If you're supposed to be with someone, the universe will pull you together. If you're supposed to go through a heartbreak to experience the feeling of loss, you'll feel it. That's the way the universe works. If you're supposed to encounter a ton of obstacles in order to succeed, it'll happen. Never question why things are happening to you and always look at everything from a different perspective. You'll be surprised at the things that life has in store for you.

Sometimes, you believe what you have
is love but it's only comfort in disguise.
You're comfortable because there's someone
present even if they're not showing you love in
return. You believe it's okay for someone to
live, eat, sleep next to you or with you...
and show no signs of affection whatsoever.
You become accustomed to that life, so you
believe it's normal for people to treat you that
way. Learn to differentiate comfort over love. If
a relationship is dead, walk away and start anew.
No, it won't be easy, but you'll walk away with
your dignity. You deserve love and happiness,
but you shouldn't feel drained or sad each time
you walk through your front door.

If you're not honest with your partner
and you keep shrugging off things that bother
you, you'll end up unhappy at some point
during your relationship. Say what you feel.
Don't wait weeks, months, or years down the
line to express what your heart is feeling.
What you ignore now will affect you later.

I remember the days I wished you would pick up the phone and call me. The endless nights overthinking about the things I could've, should've said but didn't. The memories overpowering everything I did. Those are the days I never want to relive. I know that I still want you, but I never want to feel powerless and afraid again. The thought of having someone love me with all their might and then drop me as if I never meant anything is hard to get over but I know I'll be fine without you, and I know I'll eventually move on.

Be thankful for closed doors that
you weren't meant to walk through.
They prevented you from exploring
toxic situations and from doing things
you'd eventually regret.

You moved on as if I never existed.
No more calls. No more texts. Just silence.
It was a few weeks later when I heard the news.
You had met someone new… someone to take my
place. She had everything I wanted in the palm of
her hands, and I couldn't do anything but envy her.
I couldn't help but wonder if you were making the
same promises you made me. Were you taking her
to the same places you took me? Were you giving
her my nickname? It drove me crazy until I stopped
focusing my energy on you and started redirecting
that same energy on me. You were my past, not
my present. And being happy meant not paying
attention to what you were doing anymore.

You have to give yourself your own closure.
You have to do it for your well-being because
they may never recognize all the pain they've
caused you, and you shouldn't be wishing for them
to change when they won't. They'll never give
you everything your heart desires. So let go of
unrealistic expectations and spend your time loving
people that show you that they feel the same way,
too. You deserve someone that's gentle with
your heart and that isn't going to run
when things get rough.

If someone trusts and opens up to you,
don't be a fool and mess things up by not
listening. Sometimes, all that person needs
is someone to listen to them and hear them
in their time of need.

Dear heart,

Let go of false hope.
They're not coming back.
It's preventing you from moving on.

- *Your brain*

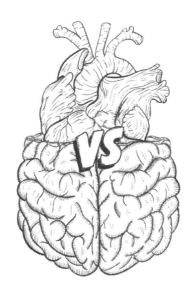

When they blame you for acting crazy
because you caught them in a lie,
you're not the problem—they are.

An apology to myself…

I want to apologize for not giving you
what you deserved. I'm sorry I didn't give you
the same amount of love back when you were
busy giving others every ounce of love left
within you. I'm sorry that you gave everything
to people that didn't deserve half of you.
I'm sorry I didn't take the time to console you
when you kept breaking down in tears. I'm sorry
I didn't do better to protect you against all the
people that lied and betrayed you. I'm sorry you
had to go through these tough obstacles when
I could've made better decisions and walked
away. But most of all, I'm sorry I didn't love
you enough when you needed me most.

Talk to yourself in the mirror
and become your own best friend.
You'll be amazed at the things you
find out when you look deeper.

You're beating yourself up
for something that you can't control.
They left you in a vulnerable state,
but this is when you should pick yourself
back up and grow from the experience.
You're stronger than you think. Get back up
and don't let them break you. Fight!

When it feels as though your
whole world is crashing down and the people
you trusted the most betrayed you, take a step
back and think about all the good things going
on. You're alive and that's a luxury in itself.
Remind yourself that this too is just a bump
on the road that you'll get over.

When you've been treated like crap in previous relationships, your mind automatically believes the next person will do the same. You believe there are no good men, or you push the good ones away because you assume they're no good for you. Not everybody is out to hurt you. It's all about learning to love yourself unconditionally, setting firm boundaries and knowing when to walk away when your mental, physical and emotional well-being aren't being respected.

Keep being fearless.
Keep pursuing your dreams.
Keep learning. Keep pushing yourself
beyond your limits but never lose
yourself to please someone else.

They may never be sorry for what they did.
They may never apologize for how they treated
you. They may never feel bad for losing you
but always remind yourself what a
phenomenal woman you are.

Sometimes, it's better to remind yourself
that things didn't work out for a reason.
You never know what the universe
was protecting you from.

You've stayed too long in a relationship
that isn't making you happy. You've lost the
essence of what love is supposed to feel like.
You've lost yourself while trying to make
things work. You've lost your worth trying
to bend over backwards to please someone
who isn't appreciating everything you do.
How much more time are you going to
waste trying to "be happy?"

You're going to be okay.
You may not feel it now but someday,
you'll feel a sense of relief while reminiscing about
this moment. You'll be in a better place, enjoying
life, thinking about how life used to be while
still appreciating all you've been through to
get to where you are now. Don't lose hope.
Just you wait and see what's in store for you.

You were fine before you met them.
You'll be fine after them.

The reality is you stay in toxic relationships
because you become infatuated with the idea of
how you expect things to be, and you ignore
the red flags because you hope things
will change. Time to wake up.

It's important to remember why the relationship
ended, why you shouldn't go back, and even
more important to realize that there's no
specific time frame for your healing.
This is your journey. Nobody else's.
So, no matter how long it takes you
to move on, do it at your own pace.

The reason you're having
a hard time letting go of your ex
is because you're holding on to hope
that someday, things will be the same again.

Stop settling for anything
that isn't make your heart beat.
Whether it be a person, a job… nothing.
If it isn't making you happy, let it go.

I kept holding on to the pain and kept living in regret because I allowed myself to believe I wasn't worthy of anything better. Not forgiving myself for past mistakes is what kept me stuck for years, until the moment I decided I no longer wanted to feel that way. I knew I was worthy of a love so real, so beautiful, so full. I had to forgive myself and be kind with my heart.

Keep living.
Keep laughing.
Keep smiling.
Keep making memories.
Breathe and feel alive again.

You'll always win against evil people
that want to see you fail. While they're busy
plotting your downfall, you're busy working on
rising above the bullshit. Love and genuine
intentions will always prevail over wickedness.

The woman I became cost me toxic relationships
and fake friendships. Thank goodness I'm no
longer around those low vibrational people.
I don't need them in my life. If they're
uncomfortable with my progress, then
they weren't supposed to stay.

You won't recognize who you used to be when you've grown into a new version of yourself. The things you used to settle for and people you allowed to mistreat you, will no longer be allowed near you. There's beauty in growth and even more beauty in finding your self-worth again.

Someday, you'll realize that everything you've gone through was a blessing in disguise. Things didn't work out the way you expected them to because you were being prepared for something better, and all the restless nights wondering why everything happened to you will finally make sense.

It'll drive you crazy to see your ex
with someone new until you let go. But how?
Stop lying to yourself and be honest about how
you feel. If you feel like crying, cry. If you feel
like getting angry, yell. If you feel like hurting
someone, write it down and tear it up. Feel those
emotions fully. Face your fear by accepting the
present for what it is. Be honest and admit to
yourself that things won't go back to how they
used to be. Remind yourself that what you
shared with your ex was good while it lasted but
they're with someone new and they have a right
to be happy, like you do. Your life shouldn't
stop just because they're no longer in the picture.
Make new friends, go out and do things you've
always wanted to do, take a trip, cut your hair…
do anything that makes you feel alive again. But
don't let the sadness consume you. Eventually,
you won't feel those butterflies in your stomach,
and they'll be nothing more than a distant
memory. Let them go.

It's not your job to rescue or fix what's broken in him, no matter how bad you want to.

Read that again.

Working on yourself never ends.
When you've reached a point where you think
you're comfortable, life will make sure to test
you and will give you new things to work on.
Keep learning and always appreciate the
lesson that comes with it. Growth comes
in different ways when you least expect it.

Isn't it time you start thinking about
your wants and needs instead of always
thinking about others? Isn't it time to move on?
Isn't it time you find yourself again? Don't you
want more for yourself? Maybe if you asked
yourself these questions more often you would
start looking for the answers instead of
avoiding them.

I was your best friend, lover and support system. You were immature at the time and didn't realize how much I meant to you. You took me for granted when I needed you most. And now, you live in your own misery, reminiscing about all the good times we shared. You regret not loving me the way you should have and all you have left are the thoughts of how things could've been, if you had just given me your heart back then… too little, too late.

Fall in love with someone who supports
and guides you. Someone who understands you
even when things get crazy and especially
someone who listens when you need it most.

You eventually reach a boiling point
where you get tired of the games and the lies,
and you just want to be at peace with yourself

by letting people go… *for good.*

Keep repeating to yourself that you
deserve a love so pure, so genuine, so rare.
Keep sending positive vibes your way and the
right one will come along when you're not even
looking. When you put it out into the universe
and genuinely believe it to be true, you'll be
surprised what you attract.

Never underestimate the power of manifestation.

No matter what you're feeling right now, no matter how upside down your life is, things will look up when you least expect them to. Better days are coming.

If I see a pattern of disrespect,
fuck it — you're dead to me.
I won't tolerate anybody hindering
my well-being. It's as simple as that.
No bad blood, no petty argument.
I simply cut you off.

Goodbye

I relapse sometimes when I start thinking
about the past. I miss my ex but not romantically.
I miss the friendship, the laughs, and our
late-night talks. Then I remember how our
breakup made me feel and how I never
want to relive those emotions again.

The biggest lesson I learned this year
is that not everybody has the same heart as mine.
While I'm ready to do whatever it takes to make
others happy, that doesn't mean others will do
the same and that's okay. You shouldn't expect
anything from anyone. Never try to force
someone to act or feel the same way or
you'll end up getting hurt.

Start fighting for yourself.
Let them go. You're drowning
while they're saving themselves.

Manifest the love you want.
Manifest the life you dream about.
Manifest the good people you want
to be surrounded with. Manifest the abundance you
want. Manifest the success you want to achieve.
Manifest everything you believe you deserve…
Believe in it.

See yourself already living that life
and then claim it!

That woman that always had your back
and never let you fall was me. That woman that
stood by your side when everybody else left was
me. That woman that only asked for your love and
time was me. That woman that would have crossed
mountains to get to you was me. That woman that
got fed up of your bullshit was me. That woman
that left because she was tired of lowering her worth
for you is gone and never coming back. Should've
paid attention to her when you had the chance.

When they try to break you,
remind yourself what a bad-ass woman you are.
Nobody can take your crown unless you let
them, and I know you have a lot of fight in you.
So… fight for what's righteously yours!

It's okay to say if something isn't working
for you. If your partner isn't making you happy
anymore—say it. If you're constantly finding
yourself staying silent to appease your partner's
feeling—speak up. If you're always making
excuses for their shitty behavior—enough.
Pay attention to what you're feeling.
You know it in your gut when a relationship
is over. There's nothing wrong in starting over
or letting go of someone you're no longer in
love with. And you'll only feel at peace with
yourself when you get rid of everything
that's weighing you down.

Some people don't deserve half the love
you have to give. You give them a little,
they want the whole plate. They use you to
get what they want until the benefits run out.
They see you as an opportunity and are only
loyal to their need of you—nothing more.
Their true colors will show when you're
no longer beneficial to their life.

The problem with goodbyes is you believe
you'll never feel that connection with anybody else.
Nobody will ever take your breath away or make
you feel butterflies in your stomach the way they
did. That your heart will never beat the way it did
when you were with them, and nobody will ever
touch your soul like they did with their words.
But the truth is, every person you encounter will
hold a different place in your heart and maybe what
that person gave you was special, but that doesn't
mean someone else can't love you and give
you what you really deserve.

You keep forgiving them, so they keep
messing up because they know you won't
do anything about it. Quit being so fucking
forgiving. Put your foot down and remove the
idea from your head of letting them back in.
You can't expect them to treat you like gold
when they keep repeating the same mistakes
and you keep accepting their fake apologies
when you know they're going to do it again.
Know when to cut the cord... for good.

If you're out there trying to be liked by everybody, you're trying too hard to fit in. How do you expect to attract the right kind of people? All you'll keep attracting are leeches if you're not genuinely and unapologetically yourself. Those that flock to you will be attracted to who you are as a person, and not for what you can give to them in return.

As you get older, your circle of friends will change and get smaller. Don't believe the motto "No New Friends" because you'll end up meeting new people that'll align with your journey. You'll let go of old friendships that served their purpose but weren't meant to walk alongside you. Your love for them will remain but you'll learn to love yourself unconditionally and that'll mean walking away from anybody who isn't bringing anything constructive towards your growth.

Just because you have history with them doesn't mean you have to put up with them treating you like garbage.

You're angry and you have every right to be. Nobody could've predicted what happened. You didn't know they were going to shatter your heart into a thousand pieces and leave you confused.

This will all pass. You won't know when or how but eventually, a new you will emerge feeling like you've never felt before. You'll feel free, happy, content, and safe knowing that you'll never allow anybody to play with your heart again. You'll finally realize the valuable lesson behind the breakup, and you'll be thankful that things happened the way they did.

The difference between me and others
is I don't give a shit what people think about me.
I do what I want when I want, no apologies.
That's why I succeed.

I fought for us more times than I should have.
I gave you many opportunities to make things
right, but everything always stayed the same.
So, I chose to fight for my damn self and
that meant walking away from you.

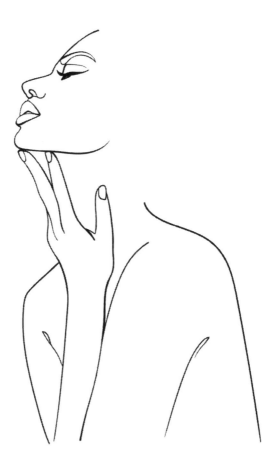

My ex used to tell me he gave me
everything I wanted and needed.
I laughed and said, "All you gave me were
headaches, trust issues and sleepless nights."

He threw it all away. Everything I thought
he was, everything I thought we were building,
everything we promised one another… down the
drain, over things that could've been avoided.
All because he became infatuated with the attention
he was getting from other women instead of taking
care of what he had at home. I saw the changes in
his behavior, but I chose to ignore them because
I refused to believe he would ever lie or betray me.
And in the end, I regret not listening to my gut.
Never again will I allow my emotions to
overpower that nagging feeling when something
doesn't feel right. Pay attention to the
red flags especially when they hurt.

You're attracted to their potential
and it's blinding you from seeing them
for who they are. Take those rose-colored
glasses off before you spend years wishing
you had made a wiser decision.

You want to call them and tell them
everything you're feeling. You want them to hear
your voice expressing all the hurt they caused.
They kicked you to the curb with no remorse
and you're wondering if they feel guilty for it.
You feel you have so much left to say but
sometimes, the less said, the better. You deserve
more and they aren't able to give it to you.
Give yourself permission to let go and move on.

You're not the same. You've evolved.
The person you once were doesn't live here
anymore. The hurt is gone. You're living
without regret and being unapologetically you.
Be proud. You've come a long way.

The last thing you need is drama in your life. What's the point of waking up and choosing violence over happiness? What's the point of feeling anxiety because this person or that person doesn't like you? What's the point of hating someone because you don't have the same things as them? Choose to be happy and believe that someone out there is going through something worse. Change your mindset and you'll change your life forever.

You want someone to give you love,
effort and attention… but are you giving
these things to yourself? You can't expect
someone to give you something you're
not willingly giving to yourself.

Normalize ending relationships that served
their purpose. Let go of people that don't make
you feel safe and aren't trustworthy.

Let go of anybody that's causing you to doubt
yourself and that show you red flags from
the beginning. Follow your gut and listen
to what it's telling you.

You're not being dramatic.
You're not overreacting. You're not going crazy.
When someone gaslights you, it feels as though
you're losing your mind. In reality, the abuser
is accusing you of being the crazy one
when they're the guilty ones.

Either you move on for good
or you stay stuck waiting for
something that may never happen.

Don't allow the person who broke your heart
be the reason you can't function. Don't let them
control your happiness, and never let them
break you further. Start living again.

You're not psychic and nobody should expect
you to read their minds. If someone wants to
make things work with you, they'll express
what they're feeling instead of playing games.
Only children play with toys and your head
shouldn't be one of them.

Let go of any emotional attachment
and you'll begin to see how ordinary some
people are. You're the reason they feel superior.
Stop giving them the attention they crave
and watch them change.

I'm proud of you and how far you've come.
If anybody knew your story, they'd be surprised to
see the roadblocks that were put in your way. It
wasn't easy but you got through them. They'd
wonder how you're still smiling when everything
around you was falling apart, and how you were
able to pick yourself up when nobody else would
help you. Nobody knows how tough it's been for
you to let go of all the anger you used to carry
alongside you, and they'll never understand all the
pain you let go of when you were breaking
down inside. So, if nobody notices all you've
accomplished, congratulations for reaching this far.

Anything that's for you will always be
for you. Nobody can take those things away.
No need to compete or prove that you're richer
than someone else. Your time will come, too.

Sometimes, you don't need closure.
You just have to accept that you gave it
your all and things didn't work out the way
you intended them to. Stop looking for an apology
from the person who did you wrong.

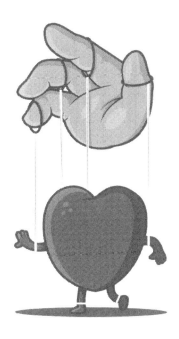

They taught you to live
without them and now that you are,
they're surprised you're doing it.
Keep going.

A little reminder…

Heal at your own pace. Don't rush your healing journey. Pick yourself back up, dust your shoulders off and push yourself beyond your limits. No one else holds the same magic inside, and that's your superpower. You're going to do amazing things; you just don't see it yet.

I hope you never let obstacles prevent you from reaching your goals. Your courage will take you places you never thought existed. Let the beautiful light in your heart shine bright and never let others take that away from you. Let the doubters live in their own misery while you achieve what others thought you couldn't.

This is for all the ones that are struggling
with letting go. The storm inside your head is
temporary. If you look closely, you'll realize that
you're breaking your own head over someone that
doesn't deserve a single thought. You're choosing
not to climb the mountain and choosing to stay
at the bottom where it hurts. Let go of your fears.
Let go of regret. Find yourself again and
remember that you're the only one that
gets to decide whether you sink or fall.

Know Your Worth

If you don't want your ex contacting you, block
them. The moment you leave a bit of an opening,
they'll keep reaching out to you… but maybe that's
what you want. Be honest with yourself, do you
want them calling or texting you because
it gives you an ego boost or do you
really want to let them go for good?

Transformation isn't easy. There will be shitty days every so often. Moments when you want to give up. Moments where your scars seem bigger than they are. Moments where you feel the weight of the world on you. Wherever you end up, always be yourself. Be comfortable in your own skin and be authentic in everything you do. The beauty in transformation is you can change directions over and over. So, if you find yourself stuck in darkness, remind yourself that there's always something to look forward to and someday, you'll find happiness again.

You deserve a love so pure and someone who isn't entertaining everyone and anyone.

Remember this every single day.

Be careful with people that come
back into your life when you're lonely.
You may find the right attention from
the wrong person and may get fooled
into believing they're there to stay
when they're only there for pleasure.

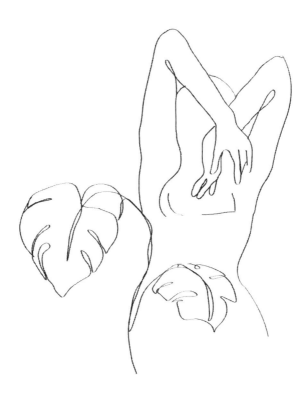

Life's too short to waste time on
wondering what other people think about you.
The only opinion that matters is your own and
what you think about yourself. So, anybody that
has something negative to say about you, let
them talk. They don't know you but there's a part
of you that they envy, so they try to diminish your
reputation by spitting lies to comfort their own
ego. While they're busy talking their mouth off
about you, keep working harder on building a
stronger version of yourself. Be wise and don't
entertain people who are below you.

Every time he calls, you drop everything for him. You don't hesitate to cancel plans with friends because you figure this time, he'll realize you're the one for him. This time he'll finally see that you're meant to be, but he never notices and leaves you feeling empty once again. What will it take for you to stop letting him back in?

You'll never heal if you keep
posting quotes or memes but
choose to ignore what they're saying.
So, ask yourself if you're putting up the posts
for show or are you really trying to heal?

When you don't lay down rules or place boundaries along the way, people will treat you like a doormat. They'll stomp on you, abuse you because they feel you'll never say anything to stop it. It's up to you to prevent people from abusing of your kindness.

I hate the fact that he knew how much I loved him, and he still broke me the way that he did. Never in a million years would I have thought that he would hurt me this way. All the broken promises and lies are what hurt the most. But I know that great things are heading my way, and this is nothing more than an obstacle in my path. I'm allowing myself to heal and giving myself grace.

You don't need to see the entire road ahead,
but you need to decide if you want to keep going or
keep staying stuck in pain. Your choice.

Unrealistic expectations will have you
holding on to failing relationships,
until you face reality.

The universe is listening. Be mindful of what you allow in your life. Whenever you start reminiscing about an old flame and you feel the urge to go back, think back at the moment things ended and the hurt it caused. Once you acknowledge that going back isn't going to benefit you, you'll feel more inclined to not contact them. What's the point of reliving a past trauma?

What's a good man? Your definition of a good
man might not be the same as someone else's.
You want someone who communicates and caters
to you, but can you do the same? Be realistic
and ask yourself if you're a good woman, too.
You can't expect someone to be "perfect"
when you yourself aren't.

You have every right to be upset, frustrated, confused… every feeling possible. Let that hurt burn you but then let it go. It'll take time to get over what you're feeling, but you'll eventually rise like a phoenix, and you'll never allow anybody to lower your worth again.

When someone expresses that they're
not interested in you, take them seriously.
You can't force someone to feel something
they don't want to. You can shout, cry and beg,
but it won't change how they feel about you.

I remember feeling as if my whole world
was falling apart. I couldn't see what good would
come out of my breakup. Many nights overthinking
and wondering how I would move on. Until the
day I realized that I didn't want to feel that way
anymore. I was tired of giving someone else
my power, so I was going to take it all back.

Your breakup might feel the same but please
know that what you're feeling now won't last.
You'll survive what you thought would
break you and you'll come out on top.

Every time we broke things off, it gave me the
chance to heal. My mistake was taking you back
hoping things would be different but all you did
was revert back to your old ways. Eventually,
I was so checked out that you didn't matter
to me anymore. I stopped letting you back in
and decided to let go of the illusion that we
would someday be great for one another.
Reality finally kicked in.

I don't question when something doesn't
work out anymore. If it messes up, it messes up.
If things go smoothly, they go smoothly.
If a person leaves, I'll hold the door wide open.
If they decide to stay, I'll make the best out of it.
There's no point in stressing on what life has
in store for me. What's mine will be mine.
If it doesn't work out, then I'm thankful
and appreciative for the lesson,
and ready for what's to come.

I'm holding myself accountable for all my
decisions. I wasn't always right, and I definitely
didn't always say the right things. I caused problems
in our relationship because I didn't want to
acknowledge that I was the problem. I didn't want
to admit that my actions were affecting us. As much
as I want to blame you for the breakup, I know there
are many things I could've reacted differently to.
I could've tried harder and could've communicated
better when we were having issues but instead,
I looked the other way and hoped that shoving our
issues under the rug was the answer to everything.
It wasn't and I see that now. I'm sorry for not
opening my eyes sooner. In the future, I'll hold
myself accountable instead of dumping
all the blame on others.

The damage from a toxic relationship
may take years to heal. The amount of stress
and anxiety that comes with it is because you're
trying to control something you have no control
over. You can't control your past or how things
ended but you can control how you react to certain
emotions by taking it day-by-day. Once you heal
from that pain, the damage will no longer be a part
of your life and you'll be able to live your life
without regret.

Don't play silly mind games or try to manipulate the person you're in love with. They won't reciprocate the same feelings you have by trying to force them and you can't make them feel something they don't. If they keep showing you they're not interested, they're clearly telling you they don't want to be with you. Respect that. Sometimes, the only thing you can do is move on and keep your dignity instead of looking like a fool trying to worm your way into their hearts.

You're not broken, sweetheart.
You're adapting to being alone again
and finding the strength within to love yourself
unconditionally. You'll overcome all the
pain you're going through… patience.

If it doesn't work out, something better
will come along. Life is constantly changing.
Even with the wrong turns you've taken,
you're going to end up in the right place.
You took all the turns you were supposed
to take. Trust where you're heading even
when it feels like it's leading you nowhere.

You're worth more than having to constantly pick up the shattered pieces of your heart. Don't contact them when you already know how it's going to end. There's nothing more you can say or do to change their minds. They've moved on and begging them to come back will only show how desperate you are. You keep accepting little because you figure it's better than nothing. Wrong. Know your worth and add tax.

Stop!

What's the purpose of talking to someone
that broke you down and made you feel
like shit? Leave your ex alone.

Don't you want to move on?

My last relationship taught me to never beg
anybody to stay. If they want to leave, let them.
If they want to make things work, they will.
There's nothing worse than begging someone
to stay when they've shown you several
times that they don't care. Stop watering
dead plants. It won't turn into a garden,
no matter what you do.

Do you ever wonder why you keep
meeting the same people in different bodies?
You'll keep meeting them until you learn
the lesson you keep ignoring.

Most of your problems can be
fixed by being honest with yourself.
You know when something isn't good for you.
You know when you shouldn't be doing things you
shouldn't be doing. You know when those red flags
are shining bright, and you keep ignoring them.

Your life isn't ending. It just seems that
way because you're drowning in your sorrow
instead of pulling yourself back up and facing
what's happening head on. You got this.
Keep your head up high and don't let
the hassles of today ruin your future.

Make yourself unavailable to people that
take you for granted and only call when they need
something from you. Master the art of ignoring
people who don't value you. Your time is too
precious to waste on other people's bullshit.
It drains your energy and makes you feel uneasy.
Spend your time with those that genuinely care
even when you don't give them something in return.

Being single is a great feeling.
There's a huge learning curve from being in a
relationship but once you get the hang of it,
a liberating feeling takes over you. Instead of feeling
as if your life is ending, you feel it opening up wider
than ever. You focus on loving and giving yourself
the quality time that you need. You get to rediscover
yourself and do things that you've always wanted
to do. You get the chance to meet new people and
discover new places you've always wanted to see.
Your world isn't ending. It's adjusting
to new circumstances.

Heartbreak sucks but you will persevere.
One moment you won't feel anything,
and the next you'll feel everything all at once.
A million emotions will take over your mind.
Your stomach will be in knots and all you'll keep
asking yourself is when you're going to get over it.
When will you heal? Stop asking yourself that
question because that's all you'll keep focusing on.
Realize you're blinding yourself from everything
happening in the moment and look at the brighter
side of things, you will survive it all.

Note to Self:

Just breathe. Take a moment
and enjoy the silence around you.
Leave all your worries behind.
Unwind and relax your mind, body and soul.

Stop letting your exes back into your life
whenever they come around acting all nice
and innocent. Most of them just want to make sure
they haven't lost your attention or want to see if
you still have feelings for them. It's a damn game
for them. They want to have control of you. The
moment they feel they have power over you, they'll
flip on you. Show them that you value yourself
and won't tolerate them coming and going as
they please. Put an end to it and stop letting
these fools toy with your heart.

Some things are meant to stay broken.
Don't try to fix things that aren't
meant to be put back together again.

Today, I'm starting over.
I'm beginning my healing process by letting
everything that's weighing me down go.
I'm closing the door to my past, looking forward
to what's coming next, and most importantly,
believing that everything will turn out right.

People aren't mind readers.
They shouldn't have to play games or have
to decode what your want and needs are.
Open your throat chakra and let your voice
be heard. Communicate your feelings
and don't bottle them in.

A narcissist knows what they've done to hurt
you. They play stupid because they don't
want to admit what they did. No point addressing
anything if you know they'll never apologize.
No point wasting your breath on anybody that
keeps acting like a child. They'll only hear what
they want to hear. Whatever you say will go
through one ear and out the other. Just accept
that they moved on, and you moved out
of their way. You win.

You should never feel like
you're begging someone to commit to you.
Whether they want you or not, never beg
for anybody's love, attention or commitment.
It's not worth the headache.

Everyone doesn't have to like you.
People-pleasing is a problem that many battle
with on a daily basis. You can't be everything to
everyone and you shouldn't want to be either.
It's your right to say "no" to anything that isn't
making you comfortable. Realize that you always
have a choice, and you can help others when
you want to, not when they expect you to.

You've been through many obstacles in your life
that nobody knows about. You've collected scars
and bruises along the way, but you've held your
head up high. You've persevered and overcome
things that others will never understand. You've
experienced things that changed how you perceive
others and yet, managed to smile every day as if
nothing happened. If nobody's clapped for you,
clap for yourself for staying strong while weathering
through the storm. Be proud of everything you've
accomplished. You're stronger than you think,
and nobody can take that away from you.

If he tells you he's not ready to commit, believe him. You can't blame him afterwards for not being who you expected him to be. If he didn't sell you a dream, didn't promise you the moon, or butter you up with sweet lies, the only person responsible for your heartbreak is YOU. I know it's hard to admit it to yourself because you're thinking with your emotions and all the hurt he caused you. But you set yourself up for disappointment by "expecting" him to be someone he wasn't. Hold yourself accountable. There's nothing worse than blaming someone else for your mistakes.

Careful who you invest your time
and money on. Not everybody is
what they seem to be.

Don't say one thing then do another.
All that shows me is that you're not serious
and you're taking me for a fool. Your actions
should always match your words. If you can't
give me that, you're wasting my time.

You want to find peace?
Stop giving a fuck about what
they're doing and focus on what
you're doing for yourself. Seriously.

Be brave to walk away
from anybody that hurts and rejects you.
Find the courage to let go and never go back.
That's when you'll find happiness.

Who are you when you're not with him?
Have you lost yourself trying to please him while
feeling sorry for yourself? Are you being yourself
or pretending to be happy just to keep the peace?
Can you be honest and admit that you're not content
with the life you're living? One of the hardest
battles is admitting to yourself that everything
you've worked so hard to build isn't the life you
expected, and every day makes it harder to leave
because you're unsure where you'll end up. So, you
settle for a mediocre life because you're afraid that
being alone will feel worse. But what if being alone
is better than sacrificing your happiness for the rest
of your life? What if things looked up once you let
go of everything that was pulling you down?

Be grateful every single day.
Change how you speak about yourself
and your life. Watch it flourish.

The universe is always paying attention.

There will come a day when I walk away and everything I told you will come rushing through your head. You'll remember all the things I told you not to do. You'll remember all the times I asked you to give me the attention I deserved. You'll remember all the things you could've done to make things right between us.

Sometimes, sorry isn't enough to
fix a relationship. You can apologize all you
want but if your actions don't match your words,
why would they forgive you? Either make
the necessary changes or get out the
way for someone who's genuinely
interested in treating them right.

You'll go through bumpy roads.
They'll scare you but every little obstacle
you encounter is nothing more than a
stepping stone, preparing you for new growth.
When it gets tough and you end up falling,
get back up and face everything head on.

I hope you find all the happiness you've been looking for all along. I hope you wake up each morning with a smile on your face, knowing that nobody is taking you for granted. A love so deep, built from a strong foundation, that nobody can tear apart. A genuine love that's patient and understanding. Someone that's willing to compromise and makes the best out of any awkward situation. They'll show you every day how much you mean to them. They'll uplift you by showing you they're there for you and believe in your dreams when others don't. I hope you meet someone that shows you what mature unconditional love feels like.

Just because you don't want to let them go
doesn't mean they'll want you back.
Holding on will hurt you and keep
you from enjoying your life.

I'm no longer apologizing for being me.
I won't always have the right answers and I'll make
mistakes every now and then. My words might be
too blunt for some but at least I'm being honest
about how I feel. I'm no longer tolerating anybody
making me feel as if everything I say or do is
confrontational because if I feel you're being rude
or disrespectful, expect me to treat you the
same way. These are boundaries I'm not
willing to negotiate.

You should keep reminding yourself
that if they wanted to talk or
be with you—they would.

A little reminder…

Never stop your healing because you're waiting for your ex to give you closure. Checking up on them, what they're doing or who they're dating will stop your growth. Let it go and move on with your life, the same way they moved on with theirs.

How long will it take you to move on?
How long will the pain last? Nobody can give you
a definite answer because they're not in your shoes.
Everybody heals differently so asking someone to
give you a date won't help you. What may take one
person one month, may take someone else a few
years. Your journey is yours alone. Nobody else's.
That's why you should remind yourself why the
relationship ended, why you shouldn't take them
back and why you should take this time to heal.
Take the time you need to patch yourself back up.
You owe it to yourself to be happy.

Sometimes, it's not the letting go part that sucks. It's the moving on part because you're unsure what's lying ahead. It was easier when you were two making decisions together. Now, you're left doing everything alone, wondering if every decision you make is the right one. Never forget that you're human and it's normal to feel overwhelmed with different emotions. Grieving is normal, but you need to give yourself time to feel all your emotions fully. Face what happened, accept that you can't change the past and allow yourself to move on. It'll be tough to get adjusted at first but once you get the hang of things, you'll find yourself breathing and living a new life. Things that seemed heartbreaking before won't bother you like they once did.

You're worth it.
Never let anybody make you believe
you're not. If they can't see what
you're bringing to the table, they
shouldn't be a part of your life.

I'm tired of being the nice one that's always getting my heart ripped apart. I refuse to feel defeated any longer, so I've become selfish in certain areas of my life. When something doesn't feel right, I follow my gut. I don't second-guess myself anymore. It's all about what makes me happy, what makes me feel complete and what makes me feel good inside.
So now, when I cut you out, you're gone for good. There's no room for excuses or "I'm sorry" because when I say I'm done... I'm done.

Always do what makes you happy.
If you don't feel like doing something someone asks you to do, don't do it. Don't ignore the gut wrenching feeling in your body because you're afraid to say "no." It'll be worse if you end up doing it and you regret it afterwards. All you'll keep asking yourself is, "What if I had just listened to my gut?" If something doesn't feel right or makes you question your sanity, don't do it. You'll thank yourself later.

Give yourself permission to forgive yourself.
You're hurting instead of letting go of all the
emotions that are holding you back. Heal.

One wrong move and everything around you
will come crashing down. Be careful who you
let into your life. Your surroundings are crucial to
your well-being. While some are out to help
you, others will drain you of your energy.
Be selective and picky of who you let in.

Never let a motherf*cker
take advantage of your kindness,
no matter who it is.

If you're only giving yourself the bare minimum
including time, effort, commitment, and emotions,
how can you expect someone else to give
you more? You deserve more than
someone's minimal effort.

Quit being so forgiving.
If they keep doing what they're doing
and you keep taking them back, you're
showing them it's okay to mistreat you.
Cut the cord. Enough.

The brutal truth about breakups and relationships.

Other Books by M. Sosa

- The Mistakes of a Woman – Vol 1
- Dilemma: The Quote Book
- The Mistakes of a Woman – Vol 2
- Letting Go: The Quote Book
- Things I Wish I Could've Told Him
- The Mistakes of a Man
- From Heartbreak to Self-love
- Moving On isn't Easy
- The Mistakes of a Woman – Deluxe Edition
- Enough

All books can be purchased on Amazon, Barnes & Noble, Book Depository and other booksellers worldwide. www.ShopMsSosa.com

Instagram: @ThisIsMSosa
Facebook: @ThisIsMSosa

Enough
2021

Printed in Great Britain
by Amazon